Donated by

Ebell Club of Long Beach

knowledge gives us wings

LONG BEACH PUBLIC LIBRARY

EYE TO EYE WITH DOGS

SIBERIAN HUSKIES

Lynn M. Stone

Rourke
Publishing LLC
Vero Beach, Florida 32964

www.rourkepublishing.com

Title page: *A Siberian husky pup spends its first day in snow.*

Acknowledgments: For their help in the preparation of this book, the author thanks Tom and Marie Kraus, Beverly Nicholson, Linda Norman, Cheryl Phelps, Carol Preble, Terry Prezybliski, and Peggy Sue Seehafer.

Photo Credits: All Photos © Lynn M. Stone

Editor: Frank Sloan

Cover and page design by Nicola Stratford

Library of Congress Cataloging-in-Publication Data

Stone, Lynn M.
  Siberian huskies / Lynn M. Stone.
      p. cm. -- (Eye to eye with dogs II)
  Includes bibliographical references and index.
  ISBN 1-59515-162-1 (hardcover)
  1. Siberian husky--Juvenile literature. I. Title. II. Series: Stone, Lynn M.   Eye
to eye with dogs II.
  SF429.S65S76 2004
  636.73--dc22
                                                        2004008027

Printed in the USA

CG/CG

Table of Contents

The Siberian husky earned fame as a strong, fast sled dog.

The Siberian Husky

The Siberian husky's fame came from its ability to haul sleds quickly over long distances. It is certainly the best known of the "sled dog" **breeds**.

Siberian huskies are still widely used for pulling sleds, but mostly for fun. Huskies have been largely replaced in big-time races by mixed-breeds known as "Alaskans." Today the husky is popular as a household pet and show dog as well as a working dog.

SIBERIAN HUSKY FACTS	
Weight:	35-60 pounds (16-27 kilograms)
Height:	20-23.5 inches (51-60 centimeters)
Country of Origin:	Russia (Siberia)
Life Span:	11-13 years

Like such breeds as Samoyeds, Akitas, and Alaskan malamutes, Siberian huskies are old-time dogs of the **Arctic**. Together these northern breeds are known as "spitz types." All of them were raised long ago in an extremely harsh, cold climate to hunt and haul.

Fluffy white Samoyeds were originally dogs of the Arctic.

The Alaskan malamute is a larger, more laid-back Arctic breed.

Siberian huskies pull sleds today mostly for their and their owners' pleasure.

Until the early 1900s, huskies were little known in North America, although fur traders knew about them in Siberia. By then, racing between sled dog teams had become a favorite sport in Alaska.

In 1909 and 1910, Alaskans brought husky teams from Siberia to compete in the All-Alaska Sweepstakes Race. A team of huskies driven by John "Iron Man" Johnson won the 400-mile (645-km) race in 1910. Huskies continued to win most of the rugged races during the next 10 years.

Just getting ready to pull a sled is exciting for Siberians.

Trained for agility events, a Siberian husky leaps through a ring.

In 1925 Siberian huskies raced 340 miles (548 km) on a life-saving trip to Nome in northern Alaska. They carried the medicine that saved hundreds of people from **diphtheria**. At about the same time, Siberian huskies were imported to Canada and the United States. (Alaska was then a territory, not a state.)

A Siberian owner shares outdoor time with one of her dogs.

The Dog for You?

Huskies are playful, friendly, and gentle. Despite their high energy, they make lovable companions. Husky owners sometimes teach their dogs **agility** and **obedience**, but huskies are not easily trained.

Huskies require lots of exercise. They should be owned only by those who are themselves active and willing to share outdoor time with their dogs.

Siberian huskies perform well in tracking events where they must follow a scent.

A Siberian husky, like its wolf ancestors, still enjoys a howl.

Huskies love the company of other huskies. Many husky owners keep several dogs, but not necessarily together. Huskies like to get together for a good howl.

Beyond a fence, or off leash, they are quick to bound after a squirrel, deer, or other moving object. Husky owners are careful to walk their dogs on-leash or exercise them in a fenced yard.

Taught obedience, a Siberian husky sits at her owner's command on a woodland path.

Huskies have long hair and they shed frequently.

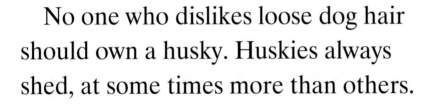

No one who dislikes loose dog hair
should own a husky. Huskies always
shed, at some times more than others.

Siberian Huskies of the Past

The Siberian husky's earliest dog **ancestors** are unknown. But some hundreds of years ago, the breed was developed by the Chukchi people of Siberia.

Siberian huskies were developed in a land of ice and snow.

This Siberian husky pup will eventually have both ears upright.

The Chukchi moved great distances over Arctic land and ice to hunt. They bred the husky as a dog for strength, speed, and **endurance**. The husky could travel long distances and still haul a heavy sled in winter. It's likely that neither the Chukchi nor other Arctic peoples would have survived without their dogs.

Looks

Huskies are medium-sized dogs with a "double coat" of fur. They have a thick, woolly undercoat and a looser, outer covering of long "guard" hairs. A husky's coat is usually a combination of white and gray or white and brown, but it may be solid black or white.

Blue eyes are common in Siberian huskies.

Happy when hauling, a Siberian husky shows off its long, bushy tail.

Huskies have almond-shaped eyes of brown, blue, or some combination. It is not unusual for a husky to have one blue eye and one brown eye.

Like other Arctic dogs, the husky has a bushy, fox-like tail. Its ears are sharp and upright.

A Note about Dogs

Puppies are cute and cuddly, but only after serious thought should anybody buy one. Puppies grow up.

And remember that a dog will require more than love and patience. It will need healthy food, exercise, grooming, a warm, safe place in which to live, and medical care.

A dog can be your best friend, but you need to be its best friend, too.

Choosing the right breed requires some homework. For more information about buying and owning a dog, contact the American Kennel Club at http://www.akc.org/index.cfm or the Canadian Kennel Club at http://www.ckc.ca/.

Glossary

agility (uh JIL uh tee) — the ability to perform certain athletic tasks, such as leaping through a hoop

ancestor (AN SES tur) — an animal that at some past time was part of the modern animal's family

Arctic (ARK tik) — the cold, far northern region of the world above and slightly below the so-called Arctic Circle that appears on maps

breeds (BREEDZ) — particular kinds of domestic animals within a larger, closely related group, such as the Siberian husky breed within the dog group

diphtheria (dif THIR ee ah) — a deadly, once-common disease that spreads easily among people

endurance (en DUR ents) — the ability to continue on in a task despite difficult conditions

obedience (o BEED ee ents) — the willingness to follow someone's direction or command; a pre-set training program for dogs

Index

Further Reading

Carroll, David L. *The ASPCA Complete Guide to Pet Care.* Plume, 2001

Fogle, Bruce. *The Dog Owner's Manual.* DK Publishing, 2003

Miller, Debbie. *Great Serum Race: Blazing the Iditarod Trail.*
  Walker and Company, 2002

Wilcox, Charlotte. *Siberian Husky.* Capstone, 1998

Website to Visit

Siberian Husky Club of America at www.shca.org

About the Author

Lynn M. Stone is the author of more than 400 children's books. He is a talented natural history photographer as well. Lynn, a former teacher, travels worldwide to photograph wildlife in its natural habitat.